Bicycle Racing

Paul Challen

Published in 2015 by **The Rosen Publishing Group, Inc.**
29 East 21st Street, New York, NY 10010

Library of Congress Cataloging-in-Publication-Data
Challen, Paul.
Bicycle racing / by Paul Challen.
p. cm. — (The checkered flag)
Includes index.
ISBN 978-1-4994-0176-9 (pbk.)
ISBN 978-1-4994-0135-6 (6-pack)
ISBN 978-1-4994-0162-2 (library binding)
1. Bicycle racing — Juvenile literature. I. Challen, Paul C. (Paul Clarence), 1967-. II. Title.
GV1049.C425 2015
796.6—d23

Developed and produced for Rosen by BlueAppleWorks Inc.
Art Director: T. J. Choleva
Managing Editor for BlueAppleWorks: Melissa McClellan
Designer: Joshua Avramson
Photo Research: Jane Reid
Editor: Marcia Abramson

Photo Credits: Cover Jamie Roach/Dreamstime; title page, Steven Crum/Dreamstime; p. TOC Bambi L.
Dingman/Dreamstime; p. 4 Jean-francois Rivard/Dreamstime; p. 5 left, 15 right Mark Eaton/Dreamstime; p. 5
right, 11 right Andylid/Dreamstime; p. 6 top Hodag Media/Shutterstock; p. 6 bottom Calvert Lithographing
Co/Public Domain; p. 7 right Public Domain; p. 8 David Iliff/Creative Commons; p. 9, 10 left, 12 left, 13,
13 right Radu Razvan Gheorghe/Dreamstime; p. 10–11 bottom Markwatts104/Dreamstime; p. 12 right
Natursports/Dreamstime; p. 14–15 bottom, 19 left Pavel L Photo and Video/Shutterstock; p. 16 top
johnthescone/Creative Commons; p. 16–17 bottom © Paul Childs/Keystone Press; p. 17 right © Panoramic/
Keystone Press; p. 18–19 bottom Herbert Kratky/Shutterstock; p. 18 Dmitry Yashkin/Shutterstock; p. 19
right Robbie Dale/Creative Commons; p. 20 left, 26–27, 26 top, 28 left Michael Albright/Dreamstime; p.
20 right Ang Wee Heng John/Dreamstime; p. 21 Cncphotographylee/Dreamstime; p. 22–23 bottom Chris
Van Lennep/Dreamstime; p. 22 left Fahrner78/Dreamstime; p. 23 right Douglas Cook/Creative Commons;
p. 24–25, 24 left, 28 right homydesign/Shutterstock; p. 25 right Doma-w/Creative Commons; p. 26 bottom
Jarnogz/Dreamstime; p. 27 right Peter Huys/Creative Commons; p.29 left Modfos/Dreamstime; p. 29 right
Elena Elisseeva/Shutterstock

Manufactured in the United States of America
CPSIA Compliance Information: Batch #CW15PK: For Further Information contact: Rosen Publishing, New York, New York at 1-800-237-9932

Table of Contents

What Is Bicycle Racing?

Bicycle racing is a fast-paced, exciting sport. Racers need to be fit and smart. Successful cyclists train very hard for competition. Races are popular among both men and women, and racers from around the world compete in events, including in the **Summer Olympic Games**.

There are three main kinds of bicycle racing, depending on where the races are held. **Road races** take place on public roads and streets. **Track races** are held on tracks that have been specially built for cycling competition. **Off-road races** happen on trails in the woods, up and down mountains, and in other natural settings.

Off-road races challenge riders with boulders, streams, and other obstacles.

Race Organizers

Racing around the world is governed by the **UCI**, or Union Cycliste Internationale (French for "International Cycling Union"). The UCI sets the rules for competitive cycling, and holds world championships in the various cycling disciplines.

The UCI also built a World Cycling Center at its headquarters in Aigle, Switzerland. Riders from many countries train there with professional coaches. The center has an Olympic style BMX track and a 200m (1/8 mile) track.

Road races are a test of speed and endurance.

Track races require speed and strategy to win.

History of Bicycle Racing

The first modern bicycles started to appear in the early 1800s. As soon as people started riding bikes, they started racing them as well!

The frames on early bikes were heavy, and early bike tires were quite primitive. The invention of the air-filled pneumatic tire helped cyclists go faster than ever before. The first race in which riders rode bikes with pneumatic tires happened in 1889.

The popularity of the high-wheeler helped create cycling as a sport.

This poster printed in 1895 shows an early bicycle race.

Popular Beginnings

At the start of the twentieth century, Americans turned out to watch track cycling races in great numbers. At the time it was the most popular sport in America. In Europe, however, road cycling was more popular, and there was a long tradition of races between cities. Even today, races like the Paris-Roubaix in France and the Liege-Bastogne-Liege race in Belgium are still held. The greatest of all road races, the **Tour de France**, began in 1903.

Much later on, in the 1970s, riders in northern California began racing on mountain trails, and mountain biking was born. Another California-born form of bike racing, bicycle motocross, better known as BMX, also started around this time.

Marshall Taylor set several world records during his 16 years of cycling competition.

On the Road

Road cycling is bicycle racing on any kind of paved road. Roads can include flat city streets, steep and dangerous mountains, or rolling roads through the countryside.

Examples of road races include **stage races**, **time trials**, omniums, and criteriums. In the Summer Olympic Games, there are two road race events, a long road race and a time trial.

Road racers must be able to race in bad conditions. The women's road race at the 2012 Summer Olympics was held under heavy rain.

The Road Bike

The bicycles used by road riders are built to absorb the demands of tough courses, usually featuring a lot of uphill and downhill riding at high speeds. These bikes need to be strong but light, so their frames are made from lightweight metals such as steel, aluminum, titanium, or carbon fiber.

Road bikes also have narrow tires, which roll quickly and easily on a smooth surface. Many racers use tires that are .9 inch (23 mm) wide.

The pedals on a road bike attach directly to a rider's shoe, allowing him or her to push and pull on the pedals with great force.

⚠ **FAST FACT**

What a ride! The average professional road cyclist covers about 25,000 miles (40,234 km) in one year. That's about the distance around the world at the equator.

The front and back wheels are close together so the road bike has quick handling.

9

Cycling Road Races

There are many kinds of road races. What makes them different is how long the race is and how the winner is determined.

A standard road race features a mass start, with hundreds of cyclists jockeying for position. Some of them ride alone, but most are part of a team of several riders.

In a time trial, riders race against the clock. All the riders start at different times, usually separated by a minute. The rider who completes the course in the shortest amount of time is declared the winner.

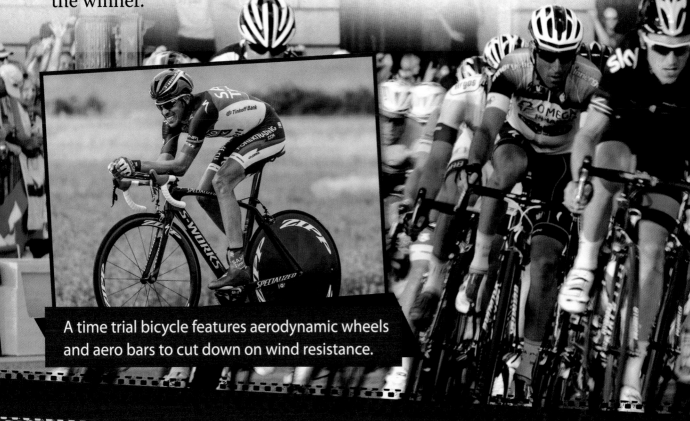

A time trial bicycle features aerodynamic wheels and aero bars to cut down on wind resistance.

In a criterium, riders compete for points at predetermined spots along a course. For example, the organizers may announce that the first rider to reach each 10-lap mark gets a certain number of points. The riders all try to finish first and win as many points as they can. This is the most common form of cycle racing in the United States.

tactics to try to win races. One of these is called drafting, or "slipstreaming." To do this, one rider follows closely behind another, so that the rider in front is blocking the air and wind coming towards him or her. That means that the rider behind can save a lot of energy by not having to ride against the resistance of air. Often, teammates will take turns drafting off one another.

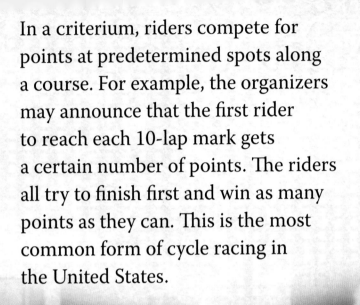

The peloton is the main group of riders in a road bicycle race.

Cyclists form a paceline to take advantage of drafting. A paceline can be single or double file.

Stage Races

In a stage race, riders compete over several days, and sometimes several weeks. Separate races called "stages" take place, usually one per day, and the riders take a break between stages. At the end of the races, each rider's total time for all the stages is added up, and whoever has covered the entire race in the shortest time is the winner.

In an omnium race, riders compete over several days, with the overall winner being the rider who tallies the most points, as in a criterium, instead of the lowest overall time.

A breakaway is a group or individual that has taken a lead in front of the peloton.

A rider celebrates winning one of the stages in the Volta a Catalunya, a stage race held in Spain.

Tour de France

The most famous stage race of all is the Tour de France. This race takes place over 21 stages every July, and as the name suggests, covers all of France. Sometimes stages are held in neighboring countries as well. The total length varies but is usually between 1,900 and 2,500 miles (about 3,000 to 4,000 km). The overall time leader in each stage of the Tour wears the famous yellow jersey and at the end, the rider with the lowest total time gets to keep it!

The rider with the overall lead wears the yellow jersey in the Tour de France.

On the Track

A velodrome is an arena specially made for track cycling. They may be indoors or outdoors. These tracks have steeply banked turns and are usually between 250 and 500 meters (820 and 1640 feet) in length. The Olympics and World Championships are held on 250-meter (820 feet) tracks.

Track races cover short distances, known as sprint racing, and longer endurance races as well. Some are contested by individual riders and others are team events.

Races include the sprint, **keirin**, team sprint, team pursuit, individual pursuit, and omnium.

The track in an indoor velodrome is usually made from pine but some are made out of synthetic materials.

Strategy

In track racing, riders use different tactics to gain an edge. For example, riders know that sticking to the inside of the track will mean they will cover less distance on the corners. They also know that they should use drafting (slipstreaming) to reduce the resistance of air.

Track Bikes

Bicycles used in track races have two major differences from road bikes: They have only one gear, and no brakes. It is also very common to see a track bike with a disc wheel, rather than open spokes. This reduces the amount of air going through the wheel and allows the bike to go faster.

Track bicycles look different because they have disc wheels and no brakes. Some are made from carbon fiber, which is lightweight but very strong.

Around and Around

Sprint racing is one of the most exciting forms of cycling. It can feature riders blazing around the track at speeds of over 50 mph (80 km/h) Riders also can intentionally go very slowly, jockeying for position until the very end, when they launch an all-out sprint to the finish.

Some track cycling races are longer and require more endurance from the cyclist and different strategies.

The different types of track racing offer opportunities for all kinds of riders. Sprint riders go fast for short distances, so they need powerful muscles. Endurance riders, who go longer distances, need to be lighter.

Sprint heats pit two riders in a head-on race. Many heats are held to determine which two riders make it to the finals.

Cyclists start by following a pacer bike in a keirin race. They use the draft to build speed.

The Keirin Race

The word "keirin" is Japanese for "racing wheels." This race originated in Japan. The riders usually race in groups of eight. They are led around the track for a preset number of laps by a motorized bike called a "derny." The derny gradually increases its speed until, with 600 meters (.37 mile) remaining, it pulls off the track, letting the riders battle it out to the finish.

The Omnium

In an omnium race on the track, riders compete in several different events, with the competitor turning in the best combined performance being declared the winner.

SARAH HAMMER

Born in California in 1983, the American cyclist Sarah Hammer started racing at the age of eight. She won silver medals in the women's team race and individual omnium at the Summer Olympics in 2012. Hammer has also won four world championships in track cycling, and in 2010 set the world record in the 3000m (1.86 mile) individual pursuit race.

Sarah Hammer has been world champion in the women's individual pursuit four times.

Team Races

Team racing on the track requires all members of the team to be synchronized with their teammates while riding at top speed.

In the team sprint event, teams of three riders compete against each other. Two teams start at opposite ends of the track, and riders take turns trading the lead every lap. The team with the fastest time wins. The race is set up to take advantage of drafting. The lead rider goes for 250 meters (820 feet), then pulls off. The second rider pulls off, too, after 500 meters (1,640 feet). Now the last rider, the anchor leg, can speed to the finish on fresh legs.

In a team pursuit race, a team of four riders races against another team, with both teams starting on opposite sides of the track. Each team tries to catch the other one, with the winner being the one that catches the other. If neither does, the winning team is the one with the three fastest times.

Riders follow each other closely in team races in order to take advantage of drafting. The lead rider has to work the hardest so each rider takes a turn.

The Big Time

The two most important races in track cycling are the World Championships and the Olympic Games. Both feature a wide range of races for men and women in both individual and team competition.

The World Championships are held every year by the UCI, while the Summer Olympics happen every four years.

Sir Chris Hoy of Scotland is one of the most successful Olympic cyclists. He won six gold metals and one silver.

The top three finishers in a track cycling event all win medals.

Off-Road Cycling

As the name suggests, an off-road race is any outdoor bicycle race that does not take place on a paved road.

These races happen on all kinds of surfaces, such as forest trails, mountain paths, and specially made dirt tracks. They are also held over various distances. Often these races feature tough obstacles like rivers or streams, rocks, logs, or fallen trees.

BMX supercross races are sprints that can last less than a minute!

Off-Road Bikes

Mountain bikes have a suspension system to absorb shocks and wide, knobby tires specially built for traction. They are usually heavier than road racing bikes.

Cyclo-cross bikes are a lightweight cross between a mountain bike and a road bike. Cyclo-cross racers may lift or carry their bike as many as 30 times in one 60-minute race so it is important that it be light.

BMX bikes have small frames and wheels that vary in size, with 20 inches (51 cm) being the most popular, the smallest in competitive cycling. They have wide, knobby tires and a very durable frame.

⚠ **FAST FACT**

The Tour Divide is the world's longest mountain bike race. It spans the Continental Divide in the Rockies mountain range, a distance of 2,700 miles (4,345 km).

Cross-country mountain bike racers compete over very rough and sometimes very steep terrain.

Mountain Bike Racing

Mountain biking is a general term, covering several types of races. These include cross-country races, along with downhill, four-cross, and cross-country marathon.

At the Olympics, the only type of mountain bike racing that is contested is the cross-country format. In the UCI Mountain Bike World Cup, riders compete in all four disciplines.

Mountain bike racing actually did not become part of the Olympics until 1996. At first, many people thought the new sport was just a fad from California that would fade away, but what happened was just the opposite. Mountain bike racing became popular all over the world.

A rider waits at the starting gate of a UCI Mountain Bike World Cup Downhill.

Cross-Country Racing

Cross-country (or XC) racing demands great endurance from competitors. It takes place over all kinds of trails, paths, and rough roads. The race lengths vary but a typical race lasts 2 hours. These races feature mass starts of up to 100 to 150 riders.

Downhill Racing

As the name suggests, downhill takes place on mountainous courses and is perhaps the hardest form of off-road cycling. Races are usually held in the time-trial format, with riders taking off at set times apart from each other, and racing against clock.

STEVIE SMITH

Canadian racer Stevie Smith is widely considered one of the best downhill riders in the world. He owes a lot of his success to his grandmother. That's because when Stevie was just five, his grandmother traded a dozen pies to a bike shop owner in exchange for a used BMX for her grandson, giving him a great start on competitive riding.

Stevie Smith was the UCI Downhill World Cup overall winner in 2013.

BMX Supercross

Riders of all ages flock to BMX supercross racing, which was inspired by motorcycle motocross. BMX supercross is very popular in the United States. Races are held for both professional and amateur riders.

Qualifying heats are called by a special name, motos, in BMX Supercross. The finals are called mains. Racers earn points based on their finish in each moto. Depending on the size of the field, up to eight riders advance to the mains.

BMX became an Olympic sport at the 2008 games in Beijing. BMX also has a World Cup circuit.

BMX Supercross riders wait to start a race. They will launch when the gate is released.

BMX TRACKS

A BMX track is a 350-meter (0.2-mile) circuit with bumps, jumps, and banked turns as well as straightaways. A race starts when eight riders launch themselves from a ramp that is 26 feet (8 meters) high. Once they launch, they may need to land quickly, or, on the other hand, they may need to gain height. It all depends on how the course is set up.

BMX tracks have straight sections, jumps, bumps, and banked turns.

Cyclo-Cross

Riders who really want a challenge and who like combining several different kinds of cycling disciplines participate in cyclo-cross. This fast-growing form of cycling combines road cycling, mountain biking, and BMX racing in outdoor competitions. The cyclo-cross season is winter and fall in the United States and Europe. Top riders look to end their season with the UCI World Championships.

Bikes sometimes must be carried in a cyclo-cross race.

Cyclo-cross races are held on courses that are 1.5–2 miles (2.5–3.5 km) in length. Riders have to be good at riding over paved surfaces, dirt, mud, and sand and at covering flat and hilly terrain. Cyclo-cross courses include jumps and sometimes even steps and stairs!

Cyclo-cross barriers are the toughest in cycling. Many of them require the rider to actually get off the bike and carry it over or around the barrier. That means cyclo-cross bikes must be lightweight.

Cyclo-cross racers must have no fear of mud!

MULTITASKING

Because cyclo-cross combines so many disciplines, riders often do well in other events as well. One of cyclo-cross's greatest riders, Sven Nys of Belgium, is a great example. Nys won eight BMX championships before moving to cyclo-cross. Nys has also raced successfully in the mountain bike and road disciplines.

Cyclo-cross racers often must navigate sand pits on the course without losing too much speed.

Sven Nys is one of the greatest cyclo-cross racers ever. In 2013 Nys won the world championship a second time.

You and Bicycle Racing

Whether you try recreational or competitive cycling, it is a great way to stay fit and have fun.

There are many local cycling clubs with coaches who can give young riders tips on road racing, mountain biking, time trials, hill climbs, track cycling, and cyclo-cross.

Of course, there are many places to cycle in cities, towns, and rural areas. Local roads and trails are a great place to start. Any experienced rider can tell you which trails are good for beginning riders.

It is a little more difficult to find a place to get started in track racing, but there are 28 velodromes across the United States.

Getting involved in road racing will help you learn teamwork and good sportsmanship.

If you are interested in racing, you can join a BMX Youth Club to learn all about it.

Racing Start

If testing your riding skills looks interesting, there are almost 3,000 competitive and noncompetitive cycling events a year, all over the United States.

Even if you never become a competitive cyclist, riding is a fun way to make new friends and learn new things.

SAFE RIDING

No matter what kind of cycling you do, and whether it is competitive or recreational, it is very important to wear a helmet! This will protect your head if you have an accident, and in most places it is against the law to ride without one.

Obeying the rules of the road and trails is also a crucial part of staying safe. If riding on the road, be sure you know the laws governing riding in traffic, and ride in designated bike lanes if they are available. If you are riding on trails, be sure that the ones you are using allow bikes, and know what rules apply for sharing them with hikers and runners.

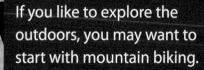
If you like to explore the outdoors, you may want to start with mountain biking.

Glossary

keirin race From the Japanese for "racing wheels," an exciting race in which racers are led around a track by a motorized pace bike.

off-road race Bike race that happens on trails in the woods, up and down mountains, and in other natural settings.

road race Bike race that takes place on public roads and streets.

stage race Bike race in which riders compete over several days, and sometimes several weeks, with the rider amassing the lowest total time being declared the winner.

Summer Olympic Games Held every four years, the global multi-sport competition that features both road and track cycling events.

time trial A race in which riders "race against the clock," leaving the starting line at different time intervals.

Tour de France A 21-stage race across France that is the world's most famous bike race.

track race Bike race that is held on tracks that have been specially built for cycling competition.

UCI The Union Cycliste Internationale (International Cycling Union), the organization that sets the rules for competitive cycling, and holds world championships in the various cycling disciplines.

For More Information

Further Reading

Jeffries, Tom. *BMX Racing*. Crowood Press, 2013.

Laval, Anne-Marie. *Mountain Biking*. Smart Apple Media, 2012.

Pease, Pamela. *Pop-up Tour de France: The World's Greatest Bike Race*. Paintbox Press, 2009.

Slade, Suzanne. *The Science of Bicycle Racing*. Capstone Press, 2014.

Websites

Due to the changing nature of Internet links, PowerKids Press has developed an online list of websites related to the subject of this book. This site is updated regularly. Please use this link to access the list: **www.powerkidslinks.com/tcf/bicy**

Index